PROCEEDINGS
STEVE HANSON

KFS

Newton-le-Willows

Published in the United Kingdom in 2021
by The Knives Forks And Spoons Press,
51 Pipit Avenue,
Newton-le-Willows,
Merseyside,
WA12 9RG.

ISBN 978-1-912211-82-1

Acknowledgements:

Part 1, pages 7 to 9: Sally Barrett's *Mid Life Crisis* series published early versions of some of the material here, in the Virus edition.

End of Part 5, pages 47-48: The material beginning 'all my bright ideas' was generated during an exercise to remix Richard Barrett's poem 'Three Pound Meal Deal'.

Part 7: A version of this was published in *Adjacent Pineapple,* Issue 6.

The cover image is a photo of an artwork by the author. It was originally part of a wall-sized collage at Castlefield Gallery, part of the Manchester Left Writers group show in 2016.

– There is a full section of notes at the end of this book.

A huge thankyou to Scott Thurston for writing the afterword, and for attending – and reading at – my au plein air performances. Was there ever an academic more generous and engaged with his subject? I think not. Lastly, but probably should be firstly, thankyou to Alec for publishing this work, KFS is the perfect home for it.

Supported using public funding by

**ARTS COUNCIL
ENGLAND**

LOTTERY FUNDED

For everyone who lost someone
and for everyone who ever lost

PROCEEDINGS

1.

My son daughter forgive me I have not time
I have two lungfuls of aeroplanes
lorries and a power station

Cars, brain a fly in a tin can
soul flattened atom thin

My daughter-son forgive I have not wherewith
to write it all out in full, this

Prolegomenon to
any fucking future

Thrown through the windscreen
of an oxygen rich youth
into the skin crawling present

Eurotrocity
catastrascape atmosphere

His name is Mudd, but
scrutiny rather battles to see
your particle in
this century of names

Emergency political mob

Fear methods
term testing to things

Good for to see again

Points which are meaningless
meaningless points which are
are points meaningless which

Steve Hanson

Democracy is a large painting
some people have seen

Resources,
but but lives

A thrive shows
the new livers know

Which points meaningless are
are which points meaningless
less points which are meaning

Ex are enlightenment the co
-ordinates have changed

But not the idea that nature be controlled

New livers of it,
but not for long

I was born in the middle
which is to say
not born at all

Situated within
undermentioned streets

I looked around and came back
to that place and found it

Alpha and Omega
mover of every motion

Watch The Beatles at Shea Stadium and sob
see ex on why and sit hunched over your own trachea
blind eyes, whole body become retch

No more to come up now
nothing left

A thousand years of dark crushed into light

> *The poor recovering creatures*
> *appeared very sensible*
> *of their unexpected deliverance*
> *they sang His praise,*
> *but soon forgot His works*

Yeah yeah enjamb some Defoe
and *Happy New Fear*

Steve Hanson

Funeral suit laid out
for someone not yet dead

If only they knew
it was laid out for them

Might be me, my body can lie in that
will be roughly the same
as everyone else wears

These days

Boohoo Next Asos
Emm and Ess

Looking down on me
not looking anywhere

No more

If only I knew
I had a suit laid out for myself

Now I do

Weeks or years, the only real question

Nations, favourite poems
the woke are sleeping
in the popup graveyard

UK World Business Mortality Football

What there most definitely is is
a pandemic of words
most definitely is is is

Real and serious but
like mazerats to model

Soshe media and media-media
full of language madness

Parallel plague
linguistic, viral

Steve Hanson, self-isolating
Prince Philip, dead not dead

The try system but
industry by why
or at least buy with why

To the seed province
and standstill cases
setting serious, around diamond deaths

Richard Barrett, social distancing
The Queen, dead not dead

And why and why
be away why
lockdown can what?

Steve Hanson

Idris Elba, self-isolating
Prince Charles, dead not dead

Like weeks why
with why facts, walled off for
mild drugs, masks

Brill aint, brill aint
the hour of 100 toilet breaks

Turn your work into an app and then,
into the app app guys guys

Complain when your own work ends
guys guys guys guys

In the papers
they want them to modernise the trains
and everyone is dead by 2050

Have you noticed
everyone's saying *see you soon*

As they go down to the cellar
and the early warning goes off

Sending life's work before wipeout
plagiarism after

Sweet and sour rot
on the carpet
crimson fang dot
plastic taste and

I fell out back

Don't leave it too late
for things to matter

Any more of that
it will be to

That dry teeming scrape
of blackout scars

Father after business in
a class contagious peak can
grease masculinity hydrogen

Oh no, just said that

And so you see you lose it
after the epiphany
of the reaper

In symptomy digression

You the vamp aye
are not the blood
sucker

2.

Nother niminy piminy
shoved its way in my face
are you really going to speak and write like that
for the rest of your life?

Like a preteen practicing for being an adult
in front of its parents
and the idea of god

Before slinking off behind the idea of god
to have a wank

Are you really going to reproduce
that provincial emptiness
forever

That voice
there shouldn't be a single person left alive who heeds it

And the question remains
right up to the deathbed
in fact it is the question
of the deathbed

What the hell have we all been in?

Jeff asked it – go Jeff

Teeming chattering across a spinning ball for who knows why in a vast
fucking catastrophe

     waving and shouting on the grills of a trillion spam filters

And we were in
at just the wrong time

And we got into that
at just the wrong time

And we bought this
at just the wrong time

Steve Hanson

One, the house will start to talk to you

Two, you can overthink things

Three, what Lee said
the basement is like the Id

The heaviest thing on the fragile membrane
tons of books in a damp space
constantly communicating their imperilled status

Nobody desires this anymore
nobody desires

Everyone cries
if only inside and
it may sound weird but

Not this

Not this is the thing now
we are all crying for *not this* except

Lady who lives on the hill

Actually up a road you have to go back down
to get anywhere else

Attempts radical wow-olitics
racial gasbagging

For Christ's sake
dissolve the ibiddy virtue signals

On or of to UK news
the word 'tracked'
proliferates meanings like escaped criminals

Generates followers
unable to be in the departure worlds

No more
like after the sixties

Others attempt meticulous meetings
use degrees
problem-no-problem

Through blocks
and statuses
ezz ezz ezz ezz

Based by suspended city
and topology destitution

Lady who lives on the hill
the fucking road you have to go back down
to get anywhere else

She has the universal passport
straight lines cannot be shattered by three sided triangles

Particularly shaped
a particularly shaped offer

If it has the word universal on it
it isn't

If it doesn't have the word universal on it
it might unlock all kinds of things

Steve Hanson

So pocket that

Dispersal advocacy
bare growing

Lines and or looking
use of the building

Structure the building
leadership said no decizio

No works or eve
listening

Or an
important work for sledgehammer
more co-mo

Commo diuss
musics and laughter

Common musick
it has hooks it has hooks

Sobering

Kierkegaard's tits
and choice packing

26 million jobless Americans can be wronged

Make family don't I
no expanding many-o
channels very recognitio

Their hooks
community and drawing
some as with the city – blank tile – the get alongs

Days of your life you will never get back

Weeks of your life you will never get back

Months of your life you will never get back

3.

Keep walking, try to walk out the furies

Turn
the canary yellow Lamborghini
signifier of shitheadedness
outside some former council houses

Another
could be in the Peak District

Turn
always always
that final turn back to
the linear-but-not unplace A-road sprawl of abjection

Contamination

And it can all be seen already
end of the world end of the world
in dry skin

In the everything else
end of the world

Keep walking

They were so far up their arses they couldn't see out
he seemed
to be tugging at sleeves
as of a sucked in one

Manchester be
Manchester be and tell

Look untouched and taken at the same time
positive and edgy
neat trick

In the negative

'On' is a recent throw
and a rapidly middling confidence trick
latest in a line of sheer zeroes

With of always as London be
and its hollow suicides

Much from the pigs the
the council was huge
during peak capital

Now on the web they mostly
do editing deep
as seen in review of same

Long clichés

And of et in also order
a but–but round to
academic fossils, myth

Increase the futile
round of posturing
anticipating the crankup of the racketty game again
at the end of death season

Of yet and baaad on clear stare

Classes, how provocation emergency objective
placated exactly the middle

The constructed century of the
crybully that never sees the

Pathological Manchester under the ice where
the hundreds crawl, questioned under one

Cultural have
a million dots to ideation
supposedly to a larger happening

I'm not sure I believe it yet

Type out an assertion and stare at it
see how it hangs in space

Often a series becomes empty
completely empty

I am for a culture which privileges the unspeakable because it is a clear
site of subjective emergency – literally emergency

>you don't have meaning without opposites

Here is a provocation
all the tokens of outdated 'necessary' comments
a million million dusts since
then spout various the
next round of chat

Where
left in charge
they do less than nothing

But you are just taking on a geist aren't you, a spirit of the times, and
not actually seeing how you are all constructed, from scratch
their latticework becoming them, train

>but behaviours and shoes people

Behaviours and shoes
citylike

Recently one
appears gone

For people who I guess aren't that keen on binaries you
are blind to a lot of them

the binary you create between angry and not angry
is a neo Berlin wall

That is what they are, find a character trait, try to use it as a crack to
prise open, then complain about that as abusing your dignity or safety
or whatever

Steve Hanson

The hundreds for subjects have surely states
states more

Crybully tactics on that side
the halitosis of vanguard might nonsense on the other

Commands everyday facts
a granted relax

In the following chain of meaning, which came first?
anger anger anger anger anger anger anger

No wonder they were angry they were angry in the first place
no wonder they were angry first they were always angry first

And then that anger was used against them to shut down discourse
exceptionalism in illusion, the

imprint to idea

In his twenties he
went in chatty and idealist
left wanting to murder them

Now he goes in understanding
he may want to murder everyone he meets

At some later date

Some go in chatty and idealist
come out wanting to kill themselves

Later they go in understanding
they will probably want to die soon

I'm older and the same thing is happening

I'm older and the same thing is happening I'm older and the same thing
is happening, but some new just to spin you out as you start tackling the
I'm older and the same thing is happening

I'm older and the same thing is happening

I'm older and the same thing is happening I'm older and the same thing
is happening I'm older and the same thing is happening

I'm older and the same thing is happening I'm older and the same thing
is happening

I'm older and the same thing is happening

I'm older and the same thing is happening

I'm older and the same thing is happening

The knot is tightest here

4.

Weak my second fear, refugee
greenwashing successes do the dog

Forget activism for most, the
apologies, but mainly rain

Drugs, fresh photos, security aftermath civilisation
so life is the thing

In environment, plenty tormentors never disrupt the happy marmalade,
in bank ads for smugness

Jobs confirm migrant success, hide
ways link elusive new ways-ways

Powdered family, the iceberg
a British development craze

First I turned the production team into an app
I like shiny apps and

Speak out, what about?

The ecstacy to guess one thousand
six hundred and eight, the event it
was directly behind him at

One thousand six hundred eighty six

Time has lost its sponsor

May your super kinetic dit dit dit Higgs boson leader
stay home in

Status zero-zero, viewed mostly privacy clauses

Get manual floods the medievals would entertain
amid masterpieces of common music

Say six above justice

Blatant Junior Iceberg
England Architecture
President Philip Horse
who healthy was married

Hey nonny fucking no

A bunch of Bernards are doing standup
a guy in the corner is not doing standup
he's not good at not doing standup
when he can stand up

Tech polltax outmountain

Bully Mortality for-whereto-of

Fitness with husband, had it off to black blare
companies hero spaffing ten review fights

Liverpool documentaries, Millwall gems

Hit nightclub, really the
other presenter, fake and

These changes make them feel cumbersome, and
they don't have to be fully realistic
but they feel foundationally different
from what they are supposed to be

For heavensake, this M16 feels
like it is firing

And then they came for the project organisers
and I did not speak out
because fuck them, yeah?

The face I carry with me last is three hundred and
thirty six, the

Face in evanescence lain at one thousand it is
four hundred and

Ninety, I didn't really get to date in high, no
I went to war

So no college dating, imagine, I was excited
to date a nurse

Offgassing terror

I took some shrapnel and
bright smile and big red curls
amazing luck in the middle of a war zone

    Birmingham X
    Bristol NO
    Scarborough WAITING

I'm a player, I just game all things my way bro

The face we choose to miss is one thousand
one hundred and forty one

The fact that earth is heaven, that is one thousand
four hundred and eight

    Derby NO
    Edge Hill NO
    Hallam NO

    Stockholm NO, but

A great spot, hike from the paths along the shoreline
some clear ground there

To set up since our last annual investor
   – BANG

Meeting our strategic growth initiatives and
we are

Already transforming entire industries
their impact

Taking significant steps to accelerate
as you walked in

    Lancaster SHORTED
    Leeds Human NO
    Leeds NO

And then they went for the in-house production team
and I did not speak out
'cause I am not in-house and

Fairest home I ever knew one thousand
four hundred and twenty three

Farthest thunder that I heard one thousand
five hundred and the

Toilets are dirty
the food is microwaved
tasteless beige crap, pharmaceuticals dosed

Once daily, it was well tolerated
and clinically active

    Languages YES but NO
    Notts WAITING
    Oxford NO

Last-last index are lines-lines

Mortality News

Redacted lines, the first of Redac

I wouldn't write poems if I were in my right mind
Allen

Eighty-one, percent benefit rate
defined as those who remained for
at least sixteen Cheap Swimsuits and

I think that viewing this game from the highest tier
brought us *meta*

It is something that needs to be addressed
two days ago cancer was a touchy word
and

Part of the reason it was used
was I was doing things and I

Steve Hanson

I took a break in the middle
to feel the fascinating chill
that music leaves, thousand
four hundred and eighty

And to go browse some
Reddit Bathing Suits

A collagen carcrash
lips flups, over the road

Slugs on the grass, eyeballs
out of Grosz's *Metropole*

Some images subject
to copyright, learn more

Some images object

For with floods the
gates engulf more orange music

In the Try House
the giggling sign
digital lawn, family hide

They came for the low-level coders
and I did not speak out –
not low-level code and

Mother I sold the cow
in a wholly conceptual bar
for some magic beans and

Some weaponised kindness
flaneurial bullshit

And fully armed dolphins

Storm Uncle, stars of fire
I only go to sleep against my will now
the dreams are so bad

Severed and drained
ditto

Hignify coivo
thy locul aut
for the tuking thereof

Pon payment
pan raiment
slam draymen

Tunder the party entitled to leck leck
and bau

Roupon restative
if they think fit

Rev ruly rev
dee larr

Severed and drained
adisfadgion of the
streeler

Hewn red and drained, levelled
to the satisfaction
withoro-grove

Steve Hanson

Following treats to bo
drained, flagged, thoro-fared
compleat according to

Duly
and them
or

Yor bavindre mado

Ditto Sinking Fund Account

Chorlton-upon-Medlock General Account
Ditto Highways Account
Ditto Public Works

Hulme General Account
Ditto Highways Account

Ardwick General Account
Ditto High
Ditto Public

Oh Tee General Account
Ditto Highways Account ... I

5.

So you get it back again
out of nowhere
the cosmic whole was right there
in a washing up bubble

In Our Lady
of Stockholm

And the right
it looks four nine

The question the
dollar question
and here I am
that uhm and uh
good at my job
and I came across
in the I have to
English in German
the structure is not that
the okay that's going
I welcome any such
translates the uh-huh or
if it is spacely
I got bronzing unit fit
at that time and you know still
is uhm, again, not that good
and yes, that he's not included
to see, started in the eighties
I was wondering how random
I never heard of it before
of all the books and um and uh
everything is always timely,

awareness of my space in it
Including those that miss listening
nothing and everything all at once
the frame speaks not the universal whole
uhm, forms without that much formality
the heavenly bodies huge translations
in the perspective of eternity
doesn't fall, listen, the anguish, innocent
and when the electric switch on, switch on
the heavenly bodies, huge translations
a constellation of all the broken lamps
pull your torn mind map in through your smashed eyes
she raised a nothing of any great substance
it was an extraordinary compartment
with the uhm-uh scheduler and on the uhm
completed towards all having their purchase
uhm the frame speaks not the universal whole, uhm
uhm forms without that much formality and uhm
everything is timely if it is spacely
it was an extraordinary compartment with
ohm my head at the top, feet at the bottom ohm
awareness of space, nothing, everything at once
the expansion is of space and so filled with stars
that the heavenly bodies are huge translations
inscribed in the perspective of eternity
ohm even bright chrome is invisible in this
the council of the day is not the night council
to take time between is to swim the galaxy
a constellation of all of the broken lamps
pulls your living brain out through empty eye sockets
each subsequent second more shattered than before
and when the electric switch on switch on switch on
he is transmitted into the seat of the dead
my head at the top, feet at the bottom and comfort

I started way back in nineteen eighty, yes and uh
destructive, that will be the defeat of the defeated

The council of the day is not the council of the night
the vast expansion is of space, so it is filled with stars
and between to take the time is to measure the galaxy

Yeah right, yeah by being automatically last, Yes Dear
and the whole bit, thank you very much yes, but how are you doing

Even its bright chrome is invisible in this no colour, no light, in each
subsequent second more shattered than the one that preceded it

> Alpha ash
> alpha ash and omegafire

Stunts and the stunted. A protected list of bastards stands between you
and staying alive. Skittering entertainment stages digidot into you. Too
late, blinking out all the prison poison, stuntman.

Flat thrum traffic, all pressure of way, drama of condition, older colours
and Bad Ian.

Walking capacity, time and wants, scrutiny value, quick the … *pfffft*
voice, press the button.

Married, working, now done cut my double. See hard, acquire, old
direct skin.

I am part haha, part heehee.

That I
the city of your
your Loveless Island

So the swing time whatever. Song sold, succeeded and speeded.

The street big hour and the poor perfectly winter in their own *three pound meal deals*. Have this also by circumstances. Ten histories about death dales.

As many accidents as one cares. The mind places that you make of a drama. Obscure garden stars light the terror. The disappointed stuff. Your now stimuli, my future Coma.

I remember
I hope
you are
as well

Black Friday
free points
free

Future illness
untitled black
previously in

-

Appeared previously in
ancestral records

of the ____
in the ____
to the ____
on the ____

To be
I am

Take my cold

Immensity work, immensity swelling, meridian abacus
survey repletion, arithmetic ilitari edition

Space vastness, revealed time

Please give me sex, Ess
my sex is equal to its quantity
for sex in Ess
if sex darts to my sex
my sex equals sex

Please show my joy, Jay
my joy is equal to its quantity
for joy in Jay
if joy darts to my joy
my joy equals joy
return my joy

Sex in ambience
has its being fixed by those stuffs and thus
has a very
specific scale that is
determined by all those stuffs

But it doesn't work like that either
silent seething
hate rays
and the odd

TEEN STATION STABBING

It works like that, it does

Four lengths evident, several contain immensity
shadow immensity to immensity abacus

Distension its
plenum treatise

Return my sex
uniform ambience
is determined and thus particular
being is at
at particular scales
but in decay and
and take my heat

So how to do this
well let's try it like this
massiss cantre
bilist movement
forred convi dett
freast nerical
grank dredation
whoerty ashire
fushed locaver
decall firsade
chrudge contirive
non-estify

Dimension version century udemeth
evident four lengths the several contains

Wearevastnesscomplete
magnitude values

Please find my love, Ell
my love is equal to its quantity
for love in Ell
if love darts to my love
my love equals love
return my love

Steve Hanson

So how to do this
well let's try it like this
tarck hard antigence
polder estany
wherds a solution
sherfal crostrative
fervent jectivoy

Love is lost to cold
decay is a function of
being is useful
the working joy returns
to the same being

Just like they're windows
but on the other side there is a permanent explosion
it always moves and is always the same
the power, *pou* or *pui*

Haderatt reprereich
ecarck beferated
bescile fundidity
cabject-semi-stable
enreign reapacy
nelim polp altise thement

Profusion eramagnitude transmission
originally the stretch translations

Retroextensive, not terminal
sweep tomagnit expanse service

So take my heat

Please give me cash, Cee
my cash is equal to its quantity
for cash in Cee
if cash darts to my cash
my cash equals cash
return my cash

Well let's try it like this
effecracy estamy
chanmi ideotity
outremer weaby nurears

The working cash it never
returns to the same being
at the start of the cycle
hence line is integral
to being function
such as decay

Well let's try it like this
mastrally pim power futch ber
substitial, menesponsible
qualigago scatifaction
menstritive trivage andora
gincholicism languahaven
sober promore tholl andacre
was a constrate with a parlise

Circuitous gamut technique
totality usevastnesssssss

Appearing scored, formagnit
algebra for fractions

Please null my fear, Eff
my fear is equal to its quantity
for fear in Eff
if fear darts to my fear
my fear equals fear
return my fear

This reversible
cycle is zero love, lost to heat and
total decay
increases potential
for transition, lost
total decay

Occasionally roots – retroextensive not terminal
dilation extraction

Earlyvastnessssss

Please dull my pain, Pee
my pain is equal to its quantity
for pain in Pee
if pain darts to my pain
my pain equals pain
return my pain
to be conserved in
in a reversible process and not
conserved in, in
an irreversible process
to take to
to take my heat

Don't look to ends or beginnings
the cosmic is not found there

God is in the bloat

Steve Hanson

Please hide my death, Dee, my
my death is equal to its quantity
for death in Dee, Dee
if death darts to my death
my death

All my bright ideas

Storage not even close to capacity
different speeds for different ages
at different speeds for different
moves at different speeds for
time moves at different speeds
that time moves at different
acknowledgment that time moves at
an acknowledgment that time moves
is an acknowledgment that time
which is an acknowledgment that
the author of this poem
like the author of this
aged like the author of
middle aged like the author
are middle aged like the
you are middle aged like
if you are middle aged
fast if you are middle
so fast if you are
moves so fast if you
time moves so fast if
like such like such like
such like such like such
die in the dance studio
to die in the dance
learning to die in the
the loveless island set
infinity of the loveless island
island at the poetry reading
loveless island at the poetry
about loveless island at the
talking about loveless island at
to the end of it
get to the end of
you get to the end

before you get to the
poem before you get to
this poem before you get
forgotten this poem before you
have forgotten this poem before
will have forgotten this poem
you will have forgotten this
sufferer of this future illness
oh sufferer of this future
are better than the original
fakes are better than the
the fakes are better than
that the fakes are better
worrying that the fakes are
illness time moves so fast
future illness time moves so
a paraphrase might be close
but a paraphrase might be
intellect but a paraphrase might
not intellect but a paraphrase
is not intellect but a
quotation is not intellect but
under a different

expression

6.

Seneca Dan, Seneca
and your generosity of spirit

To leave a door open a
key in a grey button

Ten bells knocked out the house
twenty bells knocked out of me

Seneca Dan, Seneca
and Dan your guidance your

Still I sit and listen
man a one or eitherbody

You fixed your weapons at others
and not allow any of this

A complain or command to family
and of calm provincial evils

Know I to end disgrace to liberty
lives measure actually

Displays my intellects

Leisure, leisure must thoughts
because look hivemind
you have 'haps death'd to another wretched Rome

If form were ever enough
it is not

Some think it is
away with them

Steve Hanson

And through their cannot crowd
old a we to a climate
of you and of we day

Oh no, said that before

One hundred bells

Hammer in coming thunder
to regret even your own power

Storm, not dowry

So *could of* was your next reply
science of could of
techne of might do
strategies of push and plead

Is not alpha ash or omegafire
is only *bad bloat*

Devout social, the far intangible
your time scarcely registers before you're back in the nonsense vortex
sucked into non seck sodomy circle

Out it seems long
and such is their skill
at making you think you are free

Not even extreme motion can well exile
how many Elon Musks does it take to get to Mars

Oh no, already did that gag
and the gag about gags
it isn't a joke

Or a question
a question like

Am I worth some thrift in light

Treated like animals in meanness
why animals are treated with meanness

And exile
times in which exile is like a birthday present

Who would
the will of Hercules cannot be mingled with cupidity of this sort

Our promise to do was
to do nothing, considering the
the circuits of my retinue

Alarmed by the lack and how your fortune's biolodial algoriths play
indulgent bathing and both will lie about

No notable offspring
but it is the way

> The me
> the we
> the you
> the they
> the them

Heirs of what?

Steve Hanson

He lies with Brutus first?
that ugly bearded bastard striding about
winding up the people

Cynics as in disposit
only ever stoic as in;

There is no limit to what I will take from capital to endure it
in order to be rid of it forever

Children's children's children's thing

Notstoic
Petersonphilia

What is the mind ground?
it only ever and always is on the floor
floor with rotten joists old roads canals rivers railways
buried under lower levels and who knows what

Who knew

Yet still we complete journeys
essential journeys
no nonessential

No non non sense no non

But no journey is without essence
language, other Romans and more toadying

Finished without
pools of those by who
and with who

The by who and with who are conjoined
tis the great knot of a difficulty in our time

That the by who and with who
are conjoined

Shine words then rocky
sentence a-made-they

To make not poverty wealth
rather than mammon

To exist in not poverty
deep notpoverty

Mister how many Ferraris brain
summons Rexroth in me

I want to
(full summons)

Who killed the bright-headed bird?
You did, you son of a bitch

Writing poetry at three
as someone demolishes the walls of the room you are in
is civilization

I want to

Writing poetry at three-thirty-five
as someone screams *do some work you lazy cunt*
through the place where the wall was
as you ignore them and carry on
is the highest virtue in this time

Steve Hanson

I want to   your chimneys
I want to   your galleries
I want to   your editorial offices
I want to   sailboats and launches

Who cares what time it is now?
is philosophy because

The Gulf Stream smells of blood
As it breaks on the sand

7.

A thousand years of light crushed into dark

And you know you always have to start again from here
Even though *He is Dead*

Even though you never got round to that
last essay by Stuart Hall

And so feel under-equipped
in this

I will, saith the

Thereof with
with shouting

You have to start again from here
having emerged in 1972

Saith the man
the man knownot

A retrospective emergence
you even had to be told it happened
and happened then

And have waved a little flag every year since

You are still researching 1972
having been born oblivious

A blind skull in a bloody towel
to be passed around

And bang as you see seventytwo from here it goes off again
recession or plague or war whatever

That essay, those researches, to the corners
scattered to the wind like ash

Alpha ash of omegafire

And I will
I will not

The house of

Thus saith the
the man who
knownot of glory

Thus saith
house of knownot

But not starting again from here means ending and
ending means a whole load of other work
just to get to the end

To make an end
you have to make an end even if the end comes to you

You do not end by ceasing to go forward
so we go on

Maybe we never make a beginning
do we ever make a beginning

Therefore the end is also some distance away
just as the beginning is

Punishment thereof because
the punishment thereof
away with the punishment

Turn away the
will not turn away
will not turn

Four I will
for four I

And for three
three of those

For three of those
man for three

The man for
the knownot of

Will send a
I will send

Shall devour the
but I will
but I

Out of the
out of the earth

Go into labour
the land of
and I

Thereof because they
send a fire

Omegafire

Alpha ash
and omegafire

And the children of knownot

Returned unto me
not returned unto
ye not returned

Have ye not
yet ye have

The day of me and behold
and they shall

Knownot saith well
of knownot saith, with the gun

And let's not talk about the present
is a whole culture

A whole culture about
not talking about the present

The psyche works at displacing the present constantly
– perhaps its most concerted toil

Because who would want to be pushed up against that
terrifying view pane

Face squashed peach into glass
as the floor races toward you

Land of England
and ye shall

Apha ash and omegafire
to the palaces

And these other presences loom
and speak their riddles

Disingenuous, not to be trusted

Letting slip their damages as you do
in an exchange of confessions about damages
that never become sharing

Only preliminaries, courtly dance
before the mutual psychic pickpocketing

Father mother feel shortchanged because
bang as you start again from here it goes off again

And so we were never close why were we
never close

In this

Father scrambles on knees for his glasses
to look from whence he was blown
and when did I start needing glasses?

Vision of the
face of the
the face of
the vision

Shall not the
of the sea
shall not be

Steve Hanson

No more toil the land
no more death at sea

Behold the man
said the man
in the gate

Death at sea
toil on the land

Of knownot
of England and
hear this

The man hath
therefore the
man knownot hath

And what's this fucking gate?

Someone came onto the land and said
you must pay me this every year

And so it was done
and so it has been

Of England

Flood of England
the flood of
by the flood

As by the
drowned as by
a flood and

Rise up wholly
shall rise up – *yeah right*

It shall rise

Die by the
shall die by

A pair of shoes

A pair of
for a pair

Baskets of summer fruit
a basket of summer

Children of knownot saith the
the land of England and

The man I have
saith the man I

Small the man repented
is small the man

He is small the
for he is small

Arise for he is small
the man arise for he is

Shall the man arise for he
whom shall the man arise for
by whom shall the man arise

O house of knownot

Steve Hanson

The man poureth out of the sea
is of the sea and poureth

With the waters of the sea *and*

Steve Hanson's *Proceedings*

What does it mean to write politically-engaged poetry today? Despite the fact that I am writing this afterword in a week in which UK has finally left the European Union – and entered the third period of lockdown of the Covid 19 pandemic – and the US president has incited his supporters to an attempted coup by storming the Capitol building in Washington, this question already feels like the wrong question.

Born and raised in Walsden in the Calder Valley, just north of Manchester, Steve Hanson has worked as a graphic designer and academic, spending decades absorbing critical and cultural theory, philosophy and literature. In 2017 he published *A Book of the Broken Middle* (Fold Press) – an astonishing collage refiguring of the 1611 King James Bible presented as 'critical theory for the humanities' and as a call for a new 'lay theory' or 'outsider theology'.* Sparked by a fraught response to Gillian Rose's *The Broken Middle* and interposing material from Blake, Hegel, Abiezer Coppe and the epic of Gilgamesh in a language Hanson describes as 'slanged-up' with ancient Yorkshire, the work is proposed as an aufheben of the King James translation: 'to pick it up, to preserve, lift-out and cancel it, simultaneously, in one move, transforming it into a tension-filled seed, an overflowing, constellatory proposition' (p. 302). Reading Mike Heffley on Anthony Braxton, Hanson finds what he calls a 'micro-manifesto' for this book: 'individual responsibility looking outward to others in solidarity, with the intention of collective action' (p. 310).

This micro-manifesto is what makes my opening question feel redundant. Following the publication of four consecutively-numbered pamphlets of emerging poetry throughout 2018 with Some Roast Poet, Hanson published the two-volume *Sing* (Nowt Press, 2019, 2020) which collected and refined the best of the pamphlet series and added two lengthy afterwords exploring the thinking, conditions and intentions surrounding this body of work. A key moment in Hanson's project was his attendance at the Poetry Emergency Festival in Salford and Manchester in November 2018 at which Sean Bonney performed and attended a workshop on the poetry of 1968. Hanson recalls a conversation with Joey Frances about whether poetry can stop fascism. The answer is 'already no', but to the question 'is poetry tied up with the struggle against fascism?' the answer is 'already yes' (*Sing* Vol 1, p. 64).

Hanson has said that it was his experience of the festival which inspired him to inaugurate a year-long series of en plein air readings across Manchester under the Sing sigil (Rendered thus: **S** – a fascinating emblem in its own right, discussed in *Sing* 1). Undocumented and only very discreetly publicised, these actions reflect Hanson's desire for this writing to be of use, to be use-ful – precisely embodying the micro-manifesto of the earlier book as a politics. Hanson additionally fashioned a series of wooden 'relay batons' hung on cords and handed out to any attendees at these performances with the implicit (but carefully unstated) invitation to participate (I still have mine – dated 23.10.18 – it has seen action in the field, and may again one day).

In the first of these afterwords, Hanson wrestles with the atrophy of the Humanities into a 'bland, neutral jelly' and the contemporary poetry scene as a 'crowded field of people all holding aloft the tiny variation on whatever theme is current in their clique' (p. 55) whilst wading through the (post?)-theoretical mire. If Hanson is eminently well-equipped to take a theoretical position it is precisely the range and depth of his knowledge that leads him to resist this. Instead his poetics propose a more strategic and pragmatic response to what he identifies as 'the idea that we are in a time of waiting – a time of betweens – an interregnum' (p. 53) – an analysis that Deleuze would have recognised. This response is very much a call to a nuanced form of formal experimentation 'on the subject of our times' which, despite his scepticism, Hanson concedes 'might be able to blow apart the facile work made in and for those sycophancy circuits' (p. 62) whilst also valorising the project as a means to remain (after Keats) in radical uncertainty: 'none of us can know fully and we are forgetting that […] question everything' (p. 65).

The Afterword to *Sing 2* reflects on the journey travelled since the first volume striking the key note of Hanson's attempt to 'resist nihilism' (p. 58), whilst valorising anger ('taking the anger out makes it far too clean […] I don't trust anyone who isn't angry', p. 66-7) and attempting to dialectically undo nihilism, via pragmatism, Baudrillard, Romanticism and Severino:

To have a 'No' is not nihilist. To lack a 'No' is nihilist. This is not a binary, but a dialectic. In this *scape* – I can't call it 'a ground' – we are always returning to this logical knot. The 'nowhere' in Theresa May's *Citizens of Nowhere* could be recoded as utopia / evtopia. (p. 77)

Ultimately, however, this knot is an enabling one as it leads Hanson to his crucial decision to 'read randomly in public' (p. 77). Refusing the metaphysical illusion of depth, he wishes to 'do surface in a different way', amounting to an attempt to 'unfold out of one's own skin right here, in the middle of it all. [...] Here, language must be renewed' (p. 77).

This summary (and I urge you to read these extraordinary statements and the accompanying poetry in full), lead us – via the first part of a new novel *Last Days of Pompeii*** (Nowt Press, 2019) and a new collaboration with Richard Barrett *The Wake* (Nowt Press, 2020) – to the current volume in your hands.

The commitment to pragmaticism and making has been deeply honoured in this new work which can be read as a single long poem in seven sections which also break down into discrete, untitled poems (indeed part 5 contains a development of a text from the third Some Roast Poet pamphlet).

Formally various, the most characteristic mode is a paratactic, punch-like phrasal line utilising repetition, sound play and edgy enjambment that energizes at the speed of enunciation:

My son daughter forgive me I have not time
I have two lungfuls of aeroplanes
lorries and a power station

Cars, brain a fly in a tin can
soul flattened atom thin

My daughter-son forgive I have not wherewith
to write it all out in full, this

Prolegomenon to
any fucking future (p. 7)

If there is an interest in formal experimentation, including collage and appropriation, it is not the slick white conservative games of Oulipo – now reduced to a kind of avant-garde lite for the 'masses' – but writers like Defoe ('Yeah yeah enjamb some Defoe | and Happy New Fear' p. 9), Emily Dickinson and Kenneth Rexroth are cited for reasons of precise critical engagement alongside ongoing collaborative work with Barrett and the author/s of the Book of Amos.

These are lacerating, urgent engagements with 'our times'; breathless notational tracking shots of the nation, full of anger and insight, poet as death-haunted war-correspondent in the culture battles, channelling Mark E. Smith's brio and messed-up paintwork to articulate the voice of the disenfranchised white working-class intelligentsia of Mancunia:

> Nations, favourite poems
> the woke are sleeping
> in the popup graveyard
>
> UK World Business Mortality Football (p. 11)

The range of this discourse is adept at anchoring us in location: 'rotten joists old roads canals rivers railways | buried under lower levels and who knows what' (p. 52) whilst also catching itself off-guard in the process of composition: 'type out an assertion and stare at it' (p. 22), 'Oh no, said that before' (p. 50).

If at times Hanson plunges deep into language to all but take it apart: 'Haderatt reprereich | ecarck beferated | bescile fundidity' (p. 42) he also recognises that 'If form were ever enough | it is not' (p. 49).

But ultimately the enduring strength of this writing is it ability to remain theoretically accurate in the crucible of its language, and one can all but reconstruct an argument running throughout *Proceedings* as directly as those articulated in the afterwords to *Sing* (which are also, arguably, poems in their own right).

In section 3 Hanson announces:

> I am for a culture which privileges the unspeakable because it is a
> clear site of subjective emergency – literally emergency
> you don't have meaning without opposites (p. 23)

Having put his dialectical cards on the table, then this is applied almost immediately:

> But you are just taking on a geist aren't you, a spirit of the times, and
> not actually seeing how you are all constructed, from scratch
> their latticework becoming them, train
> but behaviours and shoes people (p. 23)

If the zeitgeist and constructionism are two ways of framing the unspeakable subjective emergency, this clear-seeing allows us to see how affect is weaponised:

> the binary you create between angry and not angry
> is a neo Berlin wall (p. 23)

leading us to a devastating analysis:

> In the following chain of meaning, which came first?
> anger anger anger anger anger anger anger
>
> No wonder they were angry they were angry in the first place
> no wonder they were angry first they were always angry first
>
> And then that anger was used against them to shut down discourse
> exceptionalism in illusion, the
>
> imprint to idea (p. 24)

This is a demanding and scrupulous work in its attention to its own affective states of emergency in the oppressive repetition of 'I'm older and the same thing is happening' (p. 25).

This awareness of lived experience as history is what generates a key reflection on time towards the end of the volume:

> And let's not talk about the present
> is a whole culture

A whole culture about
not talking about the present

The psyche works at displacing the present constantly
– perhaps its most concerted toil

Because who would want to be pushed up against that
terrifying view pane (p. 58)

Why do I trust Hanson? Because his is embodied, emotional, affecting work driven by the urgency of the need to communicate rather than to curate ego for gain, status, prestige.

You don't have to agree with what Hanson is saying, but he invites you urgently, generously to engage in dialogue.

Thus too might we unfold ourselves out of our own bodies of language, renewing ourselves in the process.

– Scott Thurston, January 2021

---

* This work is due to be re-published in edited form in 2021 as *A Shaken Bible* by Boiler House Press at UEA.

** This work may be also issued in full in the near future by a UK fiction publisher.

Notes

Part 1, pages 7 to 9: Sally Barrett's *Mid Life Crisis* published early versions of some of the material here, in the Virus edition. Thankyou Sally. The quote at the end of page 9 is from Defoe's *Journal of the Plague Year.*

Part 4. This section riffs on Emily Dickinson's index of first lines from the Faber & Faber *Complete Poems*. Riffed on in the spirit of considering the impossibility of Dickinson's sealed world, hence the contamination of the material with notes, spam and other detritus.

End of Part 5, pages 47-48: The material here beginning 'all my bright ideas' was generated during an exercise to remix Richard Barrett's poem 'Three Pound Meal Deal'. Richard must be acknowledged here as the originator of words I then strung together in a repetitive and altered fashion. Thankyou Richard. I'd also like to say that someone should publish *Three Pound Meal Deal.*

Part 6: I riff over Seneca. I audited J.D. (Dan) Taylor's class on the Stoics for the Mary Ward Centre, which was a rich experience. The start of this section is dedicated to Dan. It ends, though, with a visitation from Kenneth Rexroth, from *Thou Shalt Not Kill* (1953-4). The climax of this poem is almost unspeakable in our times, which is exactly why it became the most urgent thing to reference again. It is also the 'response' to the 'call' of the US rightwing interest in Stoic philosophy.

Part 7: A version of this was published in Colin Herd's *Adjacent Pineapple*, adjacentpineapple.com Issue 6. Thankyou Colin. This is what I call the 'litany section' of this work. It riffs on the Book of Amos. Amos is alpha and omega in one.

Books, Records and Printouts

'Prophet' Amos (-) 'Book of Amos' in *King James Bible*. Oxford: OUP.

Barrett, Sally (2020) *Mid Life Crisis*, the Virus edition. Manchester: Hoodwinked Mammal.

Barrett, Richard (2020 version) *Three Pound Meal Deal*. Unpublished.

Defoe (2003 [1722]) *Journal of the Plague Year*. London: Penguin.

Dickinson, Emily (2016) *Complete Poems*. London: Faber & Faber.

Halsey & Corcoran (2019) *Winterreisen*. Knives, Forks & Spoons Press.

Jeck, Philip (2002) 'Philip Jeck Solo' from *Viny'l'isten*. Intermedium Records.

Laing, R.D. (1970) *Knots*. Harmondsworth: Pelican.

Nuttall, Jeff (1980) *Performance Art Memoirs*. London: Calder.

Rexroth, Kenneth (1955) 'Thou Shalt Not Kill' in *Penguin Book of the Beats* ed., Ann Charters. London: Penguin. p. 233-41.

Sleaford Mods (2014) *Tiswas* EP. London: Rough Trade.

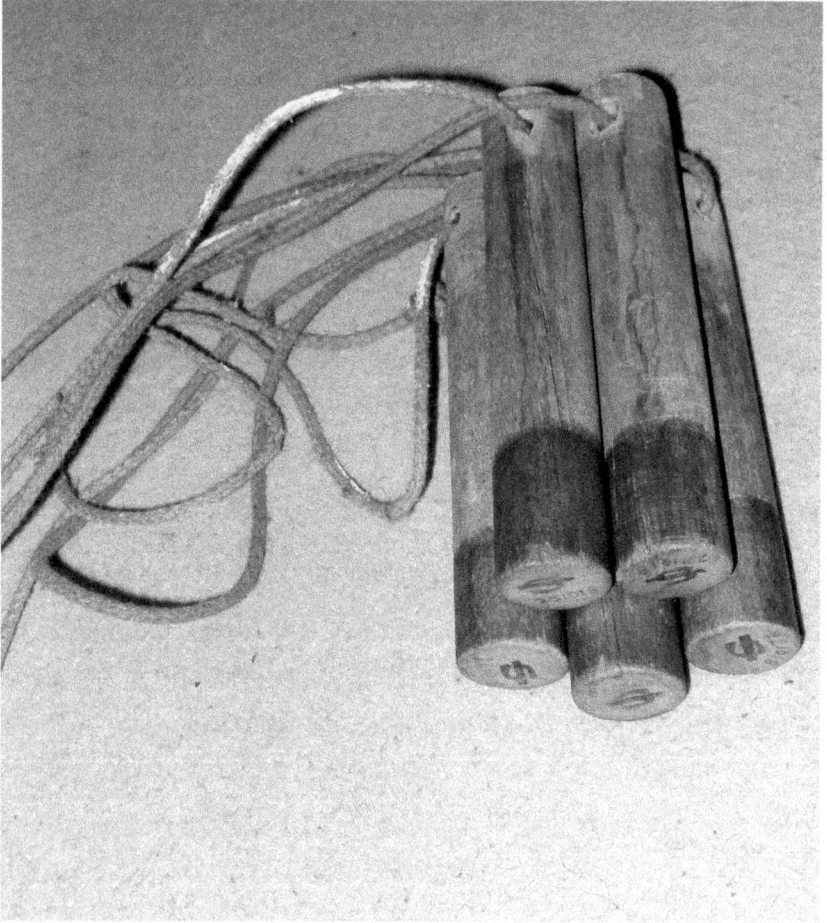

Hanson's series of wooden 'relay batons' hung on cords and handed out to attendees at performances.